UP Colony

The Story of Resource Exploitation in Upper Michigan

Focus on Sault Sainte Marie Industries

By Phil Bellfy, PhD

Ziibi Press

Sault Ste. Marie, MI

UP Colony: The Story of Resource Exploitation in Upper Michigan —
Focus on Sault Sainte Marie Industries

ISBN 978-1-61599-606-3 paperback
ISBN 978-1-61599-607-0 eBook

Ziibi Press is an imprint of
Modern History Press
5145 Pontiac Trail
Ann Arbor, MI

info@ModernHistoryPress.com
www.ModernHistoryPress.com

Tollfree 888-761-6268
FAX 734-663-6861

Distributed by Ingram (USA/CAN/AU), Bertram's Books (EU/UK)

Contents

Table of Figures

ABSTRACT

The exploitation and poverty of Michigan's Upper Peninsula and the industrial growth and decline of the Upper Peninsula city of Sault Ste. Marie are examined within an internal colony framework using a six-point paradigm developed by Pablo Gonzales-Casanova. The six points are: (1) the economy of the internal colony is structured to complement that of the colonial center; (2) the "development" is tied to one predominant sector; (3) the monopoly structure is controlled by one colonial center; (4) there exists an obvious disparity in the standards of living between colony and center; (5) there exists a repressive conflict-resolution structure; and (6) there is a tendency for existing inequalities to increase over time. After a thorough examination of the Upper Peninsula's and Sault Ste. Marie's experiences, it is concluded that the internal colony appellation is appropriate when speaking of the history of Michigan's Upper Peninsula.

NEW INTRODUCTION

This book evolved out of my Master's Thesis, completed in 1981. I have resisted the temptation to change the body of the original text (other than cleaning up the typos, spelling errors, etc.). But this "New Introduction" should give the reader some background.

As is the case with almost all "academic" work, this study suffers from a kind of "tunnel vision," given that, almost by necessity, academic work is very narrowly focused, and, again by "the standards" of the Academy, the work is very often based on obscure theory, and even more obscure research.

This thesis is no different. My MA is in Sociology, and the sub-area of this work was in the field of "Conflict and Change." This field was in direct contrast to the other "concentration" that was offered at Michigan State University, at the time: "Rural Sociology." It's not like the two fields were incompatible; it's just that "Conflict and Change" took a more Marxist approach to the study and understanding of social institutions.

I grew up in the Detroit suburb of Livonia, the whitest community of its size in the US (Detroit, the "blackest" city of its size in the US, is right next-door). In the fall of 1970, after my military service, and spending just over a year in Detroit, I moved to Sault Ste. Marie, in Michigan's Upper Peninsula, right on the Canadian border, with Sault, Ontario, just a short bridge-ride away.

I was immediately struck by the contrast between these two cities – which was a wholly different contrast than that between Livonia and Detroit. Sault Michigan was clearly a city on the decline, while Sault Ontario shared none of the malaise that infected the Michigan half of these "Sister Cities." (Detroit's decline was not yet evident.)

I was also struck by the raw beauty of Michigan's Upper Peninsula, and, perhaps, even more struck by the raw beauty of the landscape across the St. Marys River. So, while I pursued an undergraduate degree at Lake Superior State College (LSSU, today), I became deeply enmeshed in the contrasting histories of these "Twin Saults," and their stark contrasts — one declining, one thriving — and the study that follows was a direct result of that fascination and interest.

When I arrived in the Sault (Michigan), the population of Sault, Ontario, was about 76,000; Sault, Michigan, about 15,000. Sault, Ontario, enjoyed two major industrial employer — a steel mill, and a paper mill (both could be seen from the Michigan side). At the same time, Sault, Michigan, had just gone through the heart-wrenching pain of seeing all its major employers close, its population and its fortunes on the decline. At the same time, the entire Upper Peninsula was also under severe economic threat with its "abundant" natural resources found to be much less than "inexhaustible."

So, what follows is the result of that interest and inquiry — why did Sault, Ontario, appear to be so prosperous, while the "Sault" on the American side was in such a deplorable state? The answer, or so I thought at the time, was that the "American side" was little more than a "resource colony" — or to use the academic jargon of "Conflict and Change" Sociology, an "Internal Colony."

As I said, what follows is my unrevised Thesis, and you can judge its historic worth (or lack thereof, if that's your conclusion). I will return at the end of this volume with a "New Conclusion" and an update on the conditions of the "Twin Saults" along with a brief discussion of the state of the "Internal Colony" we affectionately call the "UP."

Note: The photographs accompanying this study were added for this printing.

INTRODUCTION

The fact that Michigan's Upper Peninsula (UP) is an area of serious and persistent poverty is unquestioned (Haber, 1935);(KISS, 1976). The reasons given to explain this poverty sound very much like the answer the old man gave when asked about the secret of his longevity. He replied, "Living a long time." When asked why the UP is poor, the standard answer is "lack of money." The answer is representative of the miasma that a critical social scientist is confronted with while studying UP poverty. The "explanations" of UP poverty run the gamut from "distance from markets" (Garrison, 1966) and "too many people" (Haber, 1935) to "disadvantageous production costs" (Strassmann, 1958). But "lack of resources" is never given as an explanation for UP poverty for the simple reason that the UP, during its 350-year history of exploitation, gave up a number of fortunes in fur, lumber, copper, and iron ore.

The ultimate question: why has the UP's vast wealth, nearly unrivaled in the whole of the United States, left the area with poverty nearly unrivaled in the whole of the United States? In order to answer this question, it may be wise to abandon traditional economics and sociology. The answer may lie in an analysis of the UP's historical and ongoing role as a colony of the moneyed interests of the eastern and lake states.

The outward signs of the UP's colonial pattern are evident: persistent poverty, tremendous exploitation of natural resources, political impotence, lack of an integrated economy, etc. The problem, of course, is whether such a colonial appellation would be upheld by a detailed analysis of the UP's underdevelopment. Al Gedicks speaks of the upper Great Lakes region (UGLR) as an internal resource colony. He presents a picture of exploitation in the mining sector, which convincingly points to a colonial pattern (CALA, 1974; Gedicks, 1973, 1976a, 1976b). The evidence he marshals is informative but apparently he has yet to publish a detailed analysis of the colonial patterns that existed (and continue to exist) in the upper Great Lakes region. This paper is an attempt to present that detailed analysis with respect to the Upper Peninsula of Michigan.

Michigan's Upper Peninsula played a central role in the upper Great Lakes resource exploitation of which Al Gedicks speaks. Historically the Upper Peninsula was exploited for fur, copper, lumber, and iron ore. But the reader should keep in mind that (1) the fur exploitation covered an area much greater than the UP; (2) the lumber exploitation, while devastating the Upper Peninsula, had harsher effects on the northern half of Michigan's lower peninsula and spread to northern Minnesota and northern Wisconsin as well; and (3) the Upper Peninsula supplied the majority of the iron ore exports of the UGLR until nearly the turn of the century when Minnesota became the dominant source of Lake Superior iron ore. Copper exploitation was essentially an Upper Peninsula phenomenon.

The Colony Concept

The concept of "colony" is an emotional one, steeped in the five-hundred-year history of European expansion and exploitation. Yet, due to this same long history, the colony concept can be of enormous value to the social scientist who is confronted with the question of poverty, exploitation, and underdevelopment. It is true that the historical concept of "colony" evokes images of one country exploiting another — clearly not the case with Michigan's Upper Peninsula. Yet most of the accounts of classic country-over-country exploitation sound hauntingly similar to the UP experience.

For example, Andre Gunder Frank writes of an area of northeast Brazil that witnessed a "Golden Age of Development." Frank notes that the development was "neither self-generating nor self-perpetuating" (Frank, 1972, p. 7) and this form of growth could only, in the long run, lead to a decline in the area. This pattern of growth and decline describes precisely the UP experience. Further, we see that in this type of development, the tendency for a colonial area that was exploited primarily for its mineral wealth was a degeneration into "ultra-under-development" when the extractive activity was abandoned by the colonial power (Frank, 1972).

A clear description of this process is provided by Samir Amin in his book, *Unequal Development* (Amin, 1976). He states that history shows that areas that are important for the development of capitalism at the center may "experience brilliant periods of very rapid growth. But ... as soon as the product in question ceases to be of interest to the center, the region falls into decline: its economy stagnates, and even retrogresses ... an 'economic miracle' that led nowhere" (Amin, 1976, p. 238-9). The upper Great Lakes region was once the world's major supplier of iron ore and copper, yet no thriving industrial community exists there.

Instead, these regions, in spite of enormous out-migration, have slid to the depths of poverty and unemployment (CALA, 1974). The "Copper Country" — an economic miracle that led nowhere.

Johnson, in "Dependence and the International System" (1972), gives a summary description of the relationship that reflects the UP experience. He states that dependent areas have economies oriented toward the export of raw materials, this economic system being under the control of "foreign" capital. The dependent area serves as a market for imported manufactured goods. In addition, the area suffers chronic balance of trade deficits, imports large amounts of food, suffers political dependence, and when resources begin to dwindle, the area's economic and social well-being tend to deteriorate as well. Again, while it is true that the classic colonies were subject nation states (albeit artificially created), more recent dependency theory tends to transcend national borders.

After all, unequal development within a country poses to the scientists nearly the same questions that unequal development between countries pose. Thus the nation-over-nation colonial relationship has been reapplied to examine evidence of internal colonies, i.e. colonies that may exist within national borders. The obvious impetus for these internal colony formulations is the realization of the fact that poverty and exploitation recognize no international borders, hence, dependency /domination and colonial paradigms may do well to transcend these international borders as well.

In many cases, theorists do just that. Such theorists have abandoned the tendency to speak of dominance relationships in terms of nation over nation. Galtung (1971) bases his theory of the world dominance system on the concept of core versus periphery. Implicit in his theory is the nation-over-nation relationship, but the theory has been applied internationally as well (Gilbert and Harris, 1978).

Generally, theorists have abandoned the term colony (since there are very few de jure colonies left) in favor of terms such as dependency, underdevelopment, uneven development, and center-periphery or core-periphery dominance systems. While the term colony was being abandoned internationally, its effectiveness in illuminating relationships within countries was being explored. Johnson proffered that internal colonies can "exist on a geographic basis or on a racial or cultural basis, in ethnically or culturally dual or plural societies" (Johnson, 1972a, p. 277).

If one is to accept most formulations, the term colony can mean anything from a subject nation or state that is geographically linguistically, culturally, economically, and developmentally distinct from the "mother" country — a tightly defined paradigm — to the rather loose and all-encompassing definition offered by Johnson in the previous paragraph.

Gonzales-Casanova: The Internal Colony Concept

The concept of internal colony presents a new dimension, which forces the social scientist to re-think traditional sociology *vis-a-vis* the colonial relationship and to see whether there exists within an internal colony paradigm a measure of applicability to a particular dependency relationship. First, of course, the relationship must be defined. While the colonial relationship quite possibly may be defined by as many different sets of characteristics as there are or were colonies, for this study, a paradigm must be chosen that first of all sets out a precise definition of a colonial relationship and, secondly, addresses itself to the internal colony concept.

In his paper "Internal Colonialism and National Development," Pablo Gonzales-Casanova (1965) warns against using the internal colony concept "in a vague, emotional, irrational, or aggressive way" (p.121). He then sets out to list six characteristics that define the colonial relationship. Gonzales-Casanova implies that few, if any, "internal colonies" would exist if all underwent scrutiny based on his criteria. Because of this skepticism, the Gonzales-Casanova paradigm piqued the author's interest in the challenge thus presented, and the Gonzales-Casanova set of characteristics were chosen to be utilized in this study of the UP dependency relationship.

Gonzales-Casanova's formulation has as its root the concept that the dominant power maintains a monopoly over the client region in the areas of exploitation of natural resources, labor force utilization, import-export trade, and revenue (from these activities) distribution.

The salient features of these monopolies consist of the following:

1. The economy of the internal colony is structured to compliment that of the colonial center. Specifically, the exploitation of a natural resource is a function of the demand for that resource at the center. This inevitably leads to a distorted development of colonial sectors and regions, most often reflected in the irregular birth and growth of cities. This distorted development is further reflected in the lack of economic integration in the interior of the colony, coupled with the lack of cultural integration and communication.

2. The internal colony in question has its "development" tied to a predominant sector, i.e. mining or agriculture, and to a predominant product within that sector, for example, iron ore or cocoa. This "specialization" leads to various forms of internal colonies. These monopolies may concentrate in fiscal areas, natural exploitation, foreign trade, etc.

3. In order to maintain the monopoly structure, one would expect to find that the land, water, and/or mining concessions are granted only to interests within the one colonial center.

4. We should discover an obvious disparity in the standards of living between the colony and its center.

5. Resolutions of class conflicts resulting from these disparities will be regulated by a repressive conflict ¬resolution structure (either formal or informal).

6. Over time, the center-internal colony system has a tendency to increase the economic, political and cultural inequalities existing between the two areas.

During the course of examining the UP experience, preliminary evidence suggested that Gonzales-Casanova's criteria could be appropriately applied to the UP experience. It also became evident that the history of the UP from earliest times to the present must present an unbroken pattern of "colonialism" as defined above. The history of each sub-unit would also be required to fit this same pattern. That is, the history of lumbering must fit the pattern, the history of mining must fit, the history of each city must fit, the political history must fit, etc.

While a study encompassing all of the features mentioned above is well beyond the scope of this work, an alternative approach was devised. It was felt that the history of the UP could first be examined with the express purpose of determining whether or not the UP's experience fits Gonzales-Casanova's paradigm. Secondly, if this preliminary examination suggested the appropriateness of using the internal colony notion, then a sub-unit could be extensively examined using the internal colony concept. Then, if this sub-unit examination seemed to confirm the accurateness of the internal colony appellation, the more thorough examination of the UP's history and present underdevelopment, as mentioned above, could be undertaken.

This paper presents the fruits of the first two examinations suggested above. First, there is a presentation of the history of the Upper Peninsula of Michigan along with a discussion of Gonzales-Casanova's six points. Secondly, there is a discussion of the history of Sault Ste. Marie, Michigan, with emphasis on its role in the larger UP experience. Sault Ste. Marie was chosen for this study because of its early settlement, its importance as a French colonial outpost, and its unique history as the Upper Peninsula's only manufacturing center of any consequence.

Briefly, then, we shall be examining the following questions. Does the history of the UP suggest the appropriateness of the internal colony designation? Does the history of Sault Ste. Marie confirm the appropriateness of this appellation? Let us now consider the history of the Upper Peninsula, keeping in mind Gonzales-Casanova's six points.

THE UPPER PENINSULA EXPERIENCE

It has been known for some time that ancient peoples mined the copper of Michigan's Upper Peninsula. The archaeological evidence suggests that these people were not native to the area, apparently mining copper in the summer months and returning south for the winter. The copper, thus mined, found its way into the Toltec society of ancient Mexico (Drier and DuTemple, 1961). It should be noted that during this period, other native peoples did live in the copper regions year around but had very little use for the copper. So as far back as 3,000 years, the UP was afforded the distinction of being a resource center of the vast Toltec empire. With the fall of the Toltec empire, the copper resources waited for the 19th century before they were again subjected to exploitation, as we shall see.

The Colonial Fur Trade

The Upper Peninsula became a colony in the classical sense in the early 1600s when the French laid claim to a large portion of North America. The French recognized the enormous fur resource of the upper Great Lakes region and began exploitation in earnest; so earnest, in fact, that by the late 1600s, the world fur market was glutted and the French closed many of its trading centers to reduce supply (Johnson, 1919). The lucrative fur trade was part of the cause of friction between the French and the British in their fight for control of North America. The French dominated until 1760 when control fell to the British, who in turn lost control to the Americans after the War of 1812. During these periods of French, then British, then American control, one element remained unchanged: fierce exploitation of the area's fur resource.

The first real fortune in fur was made by John Jacob Astor. In the early 1800s, he established the American Fur Company, headquartered on Mackinac Island. Through shrewd and at times ruthless dealing, he managed to control the fur trade in the entire Great Lakes region, northwest to the Pacific, and south to the Gulf of Mexico (Johnson, 1919). He easily became a millionaire — perhaps America's first — and was clever enough to sell out in 1834, just as the fur-bearing animals were diminishing to scarcity (Catton, 1976).

During the entire period of intensive fur harvest, from the 1630s to the 1830s, the Great Lakes region was the center of all fur trading activities. This is not to say that the Great Lakes land areas contributed most to this trade, for when we speak of the Fur Trade in Michigan, we mean just that: fur trade. This vast commercial enterprise, spanning two centuries, was conducted on the shores of the Great Lakes because everything moved by water — fur, and the foods, trinkets, and brandy traded for them. The principal centers of this trade were Sault Ste. Marie, Mackinac Island, and Detroit. Since the pelts came from all over the North American continent, we have no way of ascertaining which portions of the various fur fortunes came out of the UP But for the argument presented in this paper, the pattern of exploitation is the crucial matter. This pattern was summed up by a writer for the *Detroit Gazette* (of January 4, 1822):

> It must be allowed that the amount of fur collected annually and sold by the traders and inhabitants is considerable in our list of articles for transportation, indeed it is almost the only article worth note. How much more consoling it would be could we feel that even a small portion of our fur could return to our territory in cash to be expended in erecting mills ... Instead all furs which are collected by our merchants go as toward payments of debts contracted for foreign fabrics or in exchange for them, not only the fur but the money received for them. (Quoted in Johnson, 1919, p. 144)

Statehood

The War of Independence brought a new phase of domination to the UP The French had given way to the British, who had given way to the American nation. The sparsely populated areas within the new American sphere were divided into territories, the UP being at times split between the Northwest Territory and the Indiana Territory. As areas organized and became states, the UP was still virtually unsettled. The 1810 population of northern Michigan was estimated to be about 4,800 (excluding Native peoples) (Dodge, 1973).

How the UP became part of the state of Michigan is part tragedy, part comedy. Due to an early cartographic error, both Michigan and Ohio claimed a narrow band of land known as the Toledo Strip. As the dispute escalated, both states amassed their "armies" along the disputed territory.

After the very brief "Toledo War," the United States Congress asserted its authority and granted the Toledo Strip to Ohio. The Congress then offered Michigan the Upper Peninsula as a "consolation" for its loss of Toledo. After much political arm-twisting, Michigan reluctantly accepted this compromise, and in 1837 both peninsulas became the State of Michigan (Hertzel, 1976). Thus began the new phase: domination of the Upper Peninsula by the interests of lower Michigan. This domination led to the establishment of the Separate Statehood movement in 1851, a movement which survives up to the present (*Washington Post*, 6-9-75; *Evening News*, 7-10-80). Statehood brought exploitation of the vast mineral and timber wealth of the Upper Peninsula to a height unparalleled in its history, and is hauntingly reminiscent of the classical colonial experience.

Copper

The 1840's "copper rush" to the UP was the first major mining boom of the United States. By 1846 about one thousand mining permits had been issued by the government for exploration and mining on government land. But without land ownership, the miners were reluctant to make capital investments and to do much actual mining, many preferring instead to speculate on the permit sale market. Consequently, little ore was mined and the U.S. government collected very little in royalties. In May, 1846, therefore, the government stopped selling permits, and later that year began selling the land outright. Capitalists from the East, notably Boston, soon became the leading investors in the UP copper country (Gates, 1951).

The Pittsburgh and Boston Company was the first to pay a dividend, in 1848, and by 1870, when it closed, it had paid over two thousand percent on invested capital. The Minesota [sic] Mining Company paid almost two million dollars in dividends, doubling its investors' money in its heyday (1852-1856) and by 1876, it had returned nearly $30 for each dollar invested (Beeson and Lemmer,

1966). Many companies, of course, had no such good fortune and most paid no dividends. Yet the potential for high profits lured many, and at the end of the Civil War, there were thirty-six companies mining copper in the UP (Gates, 1951).

Most of these companies were quite small, twenty-nine of them producing less than one-half million pounds per year, yet the members of two Boston financial groups sat on the boards of 85% of the companies that made any money at all during the Civil War (Gates, 1951). This concentration of control continued to be the dominant pattern in copper mining companies.

The Calumet and Hecla Company, a Boston capitalist enterprise, became the dominant force in the production of United States copper after the Civil War. Between 1869 and 1879 it shipped one-half of all U.S. copper. Its share of Michigan copper for the one-hundred year period from 1846 to 1946 was 48%. By 1884, Calumet and Hecla had become the sole selling agent for all Michigan copper, and together with three other mines (all Boston companies also) produced 71% of the copper mined in Michigan (Gates, 1951).

Boston capitalists looked upon the copper of the UP as their private preserve. In 1904 two companies, Calumet and Hecla and Quincy, and two financial interest groups, those of Paine-Stanton and Bigelow-Lewisohn, controlled mines accounting for 95.8% of the Michigan output. Both companies and both groups were composed of Boston capitalists (Gates, 1951).

In light of this concentration, let us return to the subject of dividends. During the period 1846 to 1946, twenty-seven companies paid out dividends totaling 350 million dollars. The two giants of the industry, Calumet and Hecla and Copper Range (of the Paine-Stanton group) accounted for 67% of all dividends paid. (Calumet and Hecla paid 57% of all dividends paid.) The estimated value of the copper shipped from Michigan up to 1946 was over $1.5 billion (Gates, 1951), but almost none of this vast wealth stayed in the Upper Peninsula.

Instead, the profits were paid in dividends or used to explore and develop copper sources in other parts of the U.S., and in Africa and South America as well (CALA, 1974). Due in large part to this internationalization of the copper monopoly, the UP share of U.S. copper production fell from 96% in 1849 to 3.6 in 1946; its share of the world market declining from a high of 18% in 1891, to only 1.1% in 1946 (Gates, 1951).

Lumber

This mining activity also brought lumber capitalists into the area. A study published by the U.S. Department of Commerce in 1913 gives a dramatic picture of the concentration of ownership within the UP lumber industry. Fully 47% of the total UP land area was owned by 32 holders, all owning 40,000 acres or more. The Cleveland-Cliffs Company alone owned 1.5 million acres — 14.2% of the total Upper Peninsula. The biggest single capitalist was J. M. Longyear, a member of the "Albany Group." He was involved with the four next largest landholders (after Cleveland-Cliffs) who together controlled about one million acres (Dept. of Commerce, 1913).

Much of the remaining Upper Peninsula was divided among such companies as U.S. Steel, the Calumet and Hecla Mining Company, Lake Superior Iron and Chemical, and others. In 1929, the U.S. Department of Agriculture published a bulletin by William N. Sparhawk and Warren D. Brush entitled "The Economic Aspects of Forest Destruction in Northern Michigan." The authors quote the Michigan Tax Commission's 1919-20 report.

> [Because of] the destruction of Michigan forests... we have seen numerous cities and communities greatly reduced in wealth and population, industrial enterprises closed down or moved away, capital transferred to other sections while forests still remain... [the complete destruction of forests] will mean thousands of people forced out of their regular employment... the disappearance from the tax roll of a large amount of taxable property, and the withdrawal of millions of additional capital. (Sparhawk and Brush, 1929, p.3).

Despite the admonitions and warnings of the Tax Commission, it was already too late. By 1920 Michigan forests had been laid to waste. The study states that in the period between 1825 and 1925, out of Michigan's original 380 billion board feet, 244 billion feet were cut for lumber and other lumber products, while 108 billion board feet were burned or wasted. This represents 92% of the available forest. The value of the cut timber was ten times the value of all the gold taken out of Alaska — three billion dollars worth of lumber and mill products (Sparhawk and Brush, 1929).

While the Sparhawk and Brush study was concerned with all of Michigan, they divided the state into regions, so that the UP's devastation can be factored out. While Lower Michigan had only about three percent of its land area supporting merchantable timber, in 1920, the UP was still supporting merchantable timber stands on 31% of its land. In 1920, Sparhawk and Brush cite this figure as evidence that the lumber industry of the Upper Peninsula can be maintained "on a large scale for several decades" (p. 9).

This optimistic statement was made in the late twenties, yet other evidence tends to contradict this prognosis of continued prosperity. In the decade from 1910 to 1920, the total UP population increased only two percent and ten of the twelve principal cities showed population losses for this period. The percentage of males between the ages of 18 and 44 decreased from 28% to 21% of the UP population for this same ten-year period. And, although in both the tax rate per 1,000 population and a per capita breakdown of those taxes showed the UP to be the most heavily taxed region of the state, illiteracy was the highest in the state, and the roads were the worst.

Farming, which utilized the cut-over regions of southern Michigan, could never be expected to take hold in the UP because "it is doubtful if... there is any known way of making (the cut-over lands of the UP) profitable to the farmer" (Sparhawk and Brush, 1929, p. 71-72). The authors of the USDA study offer perhaps the most eloquent statement supporting this paper's exploration of the colonial aspects of lumbering in northern Michigan:

> The removal of the forests in most parts of northern Michigan... has not been followed by the utilization of a considerable proportion of the land, either for farming or for anything else. Comparatively few of the loggers were permanent settlers; most of them came north in the winter to earn cash wages, which they either "blew in" at the end of the season or took south to live on while developing farms in southern Michigan, Ohio, or Indiana. The greater part of the supplies and equipment consumed in exploiting the forests was produced by farms and factories in other regions. Few of the fortunes gained from lumbering were utilized for the benefit of the timber region itself. For the most part, they were invested in other businesses, or reinvested in stripping the timber from other States. Even the towns and cities that grew up around sawmills and wood-working factories were mostly only temporary centers of trade and industry, doomed to

inevitable decline, if not complete extinction, with the passing of the forests which supported them.

The conclusion is inevitable that the exploitation of the forest wealth of this great territory, embracing an area almost as large as the State of Indiana, has not been of lasting benefit to the region itself. On the contrary, northern Michigan has been impoverished for the benefit of other parts of the country, and its productiveness has been so impaired that not for many years to come can it support as many people and industries as were in the region 30 years ago (1900). (Sparhawk and Brush, 1929, pp. 12-20)

Using Sparhawk and Brush's figures it is estimated that the UP's share of the lumber value taken from Michigan forests is about one billion dollars. Again we see, as was the case with fur and copper, that almost none of the money remained in the UP and only limited use was made of the lumber in situ: "export" was the name of the game. In fact, during the height of the lumbering boom from 1880 to 1890 Michigan shipped four and one-half times as much lumber as it consumed. Yet by 1912, Michigan was a net importer of lumber (Sparhawk and Brush, 1929).

Iron

Iron mining in the UP follows much the same pattern that was evident in the copper industry: control by outside interests and no secondary industries to utilize the ore in the UP The first mining company to ship iron ore (in 1850) was the Jackson Mining Company, organized by capitalists from Jackson, Michigan, and soon bought out by Pennsylvania financiers (Besson and Lemmer, 1966). From the very beginning the control of Michigan iron mines was centered in the lower lake ports.

Of the 96 mines in the UP in 1950, two-thirds were owned by companies headquartered in Cleveland; 25% were in Chicago and Pittsburgh. The one mining company that was headquartered in Michigan, the North Range Mining Company of Negaunee, Michigan, owned four mines. Together these four mines shipped only 1.7% of all ore shipped from the UP before 1950 (Lake Superior Iron Ore Association (LSIOA), 1952).

The concentration of control is duplicated by the concentration of consumption. Within the states of Pennsylvania, Ohio, Indiana, and

Illinois were 77% of all blast furnaces dependent, in 1950, on iron ore from the Lake Superior region. Unfortunately data for consumption does not differentiate the source of iron ore; in 1950, Minnesota shipped 81.7% of the total ore shipped; Michigan shipped 16.2%, and Wisconsin, 2.1% (LSIOA, 1952). Obviously, by 1950, Michigan iron ore was playing a poor second fiddle to Minnesota ore (In 1900, the ratio was 47.6 for Michigan to 49.5 for Minnesota.)

However, this does not weaken the arguments with which we are presently concerned, i.e., that the UP iron ore industry is mightily controlled by the interests of one center and that local control and utilization is virtually nonexistent. The author did find an account of one attempt to produce pig iron in the UP utilizing the available resources. This occurred in the 1870s, but output never reached even five percent of the U.S. total and the operation was abandoned. Had attempts such as these been repeated, perhaps these secondary industrial concerns could have helped to break the colonial extraction pattern we have seen thus far.

The Gonzales-Casanova Paradigm

The history of the UP fur trade, lumbering, and copper and iron mining shows a definite pattern of exploitation, which conforms to the patterns established in Gonzales-Casanova's first three points. Concerning the first point, the economy of the UP, woefully underdeveloped, has always been directly tied to resource extraction for the benefit of outside interests. The lack of economic integration is obvious; the exploitation returned nothing to the UP; no secondary industries arose to utilize the natural resources of the area. Also, the irregular birth, growth, and decline of its cities is phenomenal. When comparing the 1970 population of cities to the 1930 figures, 71% of these places show a declining population (Rodefeld, 1976).

Gonzales-Casanova's second point comes even closer to the UP experience. The "development" of the UP has always been tied to one predominant factor resource extraction. The fur trade was finished by the time copper and iron ore mining began in the 1840s. Mining soon dominated the UP economic picture. The UP was the most important source of both iron ore and copper up to and during the Civil War (Beeson and Lemmer, 1966). While both copper and iron ore mining continued to prosper into the 1900s, the importance of these mining fields diminished.

By the mid-1880s Michigan's share of U. S. copper production dropped below 50%. Prior to 1884 Michigan iron ore was the only ore shipped from the Great Lakes region; yet by 1901, Minnesota was shipping more ore than the Michigan fields. In Gonzales-Casanova's paradigm one should find that concessions granted in the exploitative process will be granted to interests in one colonial center. In copper mining, we have seen that Boston capitalists were in complete control: by 1918, three Boston companies controlled 92% of Michigan output. In the iron ore industry, we have seen that 92% of Michigan mines were controlled by either Cleveland, Chicago, or Pittsburgh interests (in 1950).

The Post-World War I Upper Peninsula

Before turning to the last three points in Gonzales-Casanova's paradigm, the history of the UP should be explored further. The great lumbering boom lasted from about 1870 to about 1905. The best year for iron ore was 1916 when 20.5 million tons were shipped. Coincidentally, 1916 was copper's best year: 266.8 million pounds of copper were shipped (LSIOA, 1952; Sparhawk and Brush, 1929; Gates, 1951). The expansion of the U.S. economy for World War I was a short respite in the decline which began about 1909 in copper and iron ore mining. After the war, production continued to decline and when the Depression came, it found an already depressing scene. During the early 1930s, the Depression era, the number of UP families on relief was about 33%, compared to 17% for the rest of Michigan. In copper mining Keweenaw County, three out of four families were on relief and eight of the fifteen UP counties had relief loads of over 40%. At this time, only one out of forty iron mines in Dickinson County was operating. Mining employment in Keweenaw County dropped from 6,700 in 1930 to 2,071 in 1933.

The State Relief Administrator stated that "at least 50,000 persons must eventually move (out of the UP)... or remain permanently dependent" (Haber, 1935, p. 10). The expansion of the economy for World War II also failed to reverse the Upper Peninsula's downward slide. Unemployment in the copper counties was 39% in 1940, and the area's share of U.S. copper production dropped to 4.2% by 1944 (Gates, 1951).

In 1920, there were 150 operating iron mines; in 1959, 30 mines; in 1965, 15 mines; and by 1976, there were only six iron mines operating in the UP In the copper industry, from a peak of 36 mines, production dropped to ten mines in 1959, two in 1976 (Wall Street Journal, 1964; M.D.N.R., 1976), and only one today (1981). The total extractive work force of the UP fell from 47,486 in 1930 to 9,998 in 1970, a drop of nearly 80%. And while the rest of Michigan saw a population growth of 89% from 1930 to 1970, the Upper Peninsula's population actually declined by 4.5% (Rodefeld, 1976). Between 1950 and 1960, the upper Great Lakes region as a whole lost 61% of its 20- to 24-year-old population and 42% of its 25- to 29-year-olds (Loomis and Wirth, 1967).

This migration of working-age persons created a dependency ratio that underscores the persistent economic woes of the UP During this period, the Upper Peninsula city of Sault Ste. Marie showed a dependency ratio of 100:116, which compares to a ratio of 100:74 for urban Michigan (ratio formed as follows: ages 20 to 64: all others) (Thaden and Moots, 1960). In 1960, it was estimated that the UP had a 30.7% unemployment rate, compared to a 16.6% rate for the Appalachian region (N.M.U., 1965).

These unemployment and population figures do not tell the whole story. Using the Appalachian region as the basis for comparison, the UP's standard of living can be shown to have been worse in most respects during the 1960s. The UP per capita income was slightly less than Appalachia's; labor force participation was about ten to twelve percent less.

About one quarter of the UP's adult population had a tenth grade or better education, compared to about one third for Appalachia, and the UP housing quality was considerably worse than Appalachia's (N.M.U., 1965). Although the preceding data are from a 1965 study, the author has found no evidence to suggest that the trends have not continued through the 1970s. With the increasing deterioration of the UP's economy since the early 1960s, and the continual loss of population, the situation most probably has continued to worsen.

A study called "Upper Midwest Commodity Flows, 1958," by Bruce F. Duncombe (1962), isolated the UP trade picture and delineated its trade relations with other areas of the U.S. It is worthwhile to discuss some background to this study before discussing the results themselves.

The Upper Peninsula is included in the Ninth Federal Reserve Bank District (Minneapolis), which is oriented toward agriculture. The rest of Michigan is in the Seventh District (Chicago), which has a greater orientation toward industry. (This split has helped to insure a lack of financial expertise and backing necessary for industrial development in the UP (N.M.D., 1962). Due to this split of the Michigan peninsulas, the UP was included in the Duncombe study along with Montana, North and South Dakota, Minnesota, and the twenty-six northwest counties of Wisconsin.

These areas comprise the Ninth Federal Reserve Board District. The bottom line of the study shows a $32.5 million "balance of trade" deficit for the UP for the year of 1958. The elements of this trade deficit are illustrative of the dependency pattern of the UP trade and economic activities.

In the import column we find that the UP must import 98% of its textile products and apparel, 97% of its transportation equipment, 85% of its furniture and fixtures, 68% of its meat consumption, 42% of its dairy products consumption, and over 60% of other food consumption. In spite of the UP's vast timber resources, it imports 98% of its paper and allied products and 52% of its lumber needs. And, although its iron and copper resources are enormous, it imports 75% of its fabricated metal products.

The Upper Peninsula exports 100% of its iron ore, 100% of its copper, 99% of its paper and allied products, 92% of its furniture and fixture production, 80% of its non-metallic minerals, 72% of its lumber and wood products, and 54% of its dairy products. If we compare the exports and imports, we see that while the UP is exporting a large proportion of certain products, it is at the same time importing these same products (paper, lumber, dairy and textile products, furniture). It would be unfair to assume (for example) that the paper exported is the same type and grade as the paper that is imported, yet it should be obvious that local industry is not serving the needs of the Upper Peninsula, but serving outside corporate interests, centered mainly in the Lake States and in the East (all import-export data from Duncombe, 1962).

In politics, the affairs of the UP show the same control by outside interests that is present in trade and economics. The state and federal governments can and do ignore the UP's needs. The winter navigation problems of the eastern Upper Peninsula, the possibility of uranium mining, the ongoing Seafarer-ELF controversy, the (successful) fight to keep lower Michigan's toxic waste out of Chippewa County, and state "wetlands" legislation provide recent examples. Because of its low population densities, the Upper Peninsula's problems are overshadowed by the representation of Michigan's largely urban and industrial population.

It would be useful to explain the preceding problems within a politics-versus-development paradigm. The fight to keep a toxic waste incinerator out of Chippewa County provides a case in point. Due to the closing of Kincheloe Air Force Base in 1977, Chippewa County's economy was in a shambles. (This will be discussed at some length later in this paper) The State of Michigan had hoped the depressed economy of the area would allow them to install a toxic waste incinerator at the former Air Force Base without public dissent. This incinerator was to dispose of the wastes for all of Michigan and possibly for other parts of the Midwest as well (Evening News, 11-18-77).

The incinerator had many supporters, almost all of whom viewed any industrial development as desirable. New industry meant new jobs and job creation in the UP is considered a sacred goal. Yet opposition to the incinerator spread widely and swiftly. A meeting was called (by this author) to organize the opposition; four days later over three thousand signatures had been collected in a county with about 30,000 people. The County Commission voted four to two to oppose locating the incinerator in Chippewa County.

This case is representative of a host of conflicts confronting the UP Almost all of the "projects" suggested for the UP are viewed by many as being designed to aid outside interests, most often to the detriment of the UP residents and their environment. Winter navigation — that is, year-round shipping on the Great Lakes — is opposed in part by those who dislike the idea of federal subsidies for the iron ore industry. State "wetlands" legislation was opposed in part by those who saw the legislation as an attempt to force curtailment of the logging and mining industries while assuring that downstate interests would keep the UP in the position of a virtual state park for Lower Peninsula tourists.

The situations that many UP residents see as problems with state and federal governments are far from resolved and the UP's small population makes it hard for these people to be heard. Many other aspects of the political landscape create additional problems for local governments.

The state and federal governments own over 30% of the UP total UP land area, and nearly 10% more is owned by six companies (Smith, 1974). The land owned by these lumber and mining interests is nearly tax-exempt. Michigan Public Act 218 of 1970 exempts certified commercial forests from the *ad valorem* tax rolls; Public Act 66 of 1963 does the same thing for iron ore deposits, and Public Act 68 of 1963 exempts copper ore deposits (Smith, 1974).

Coupled with the fact that there is virtually no industrial tax base, these laws have obviously resulted in a situation in which the local governments lack the resources needed to provide basic services to people living in the area. Another result is the continual battle over rising taxes as poverty and unemployment create greater social costs with fewer and fewer resources to meet those costs.

The Gonzales-Casanova Paradigm: The Final Three Points

We are now in a position to examine the final three points in the Gonzales-Casanova paradigm. The comparison of the UP living standards to those of Appalachia showed that in many respects the UP's living standards were below those of Appalachia, an area of unquestioned poverty. So it is obvious that a comparison of UP living standards to those evidenced in those cities identified as centers of UP control — Boston, Pittsburgh, Cleveland, and Chicago — would place the UP in a very disadvantaged position *vis-a-vis* these centers.

Gonzales-Casanova's fifth point, that there exists a formal or informal repressive structure for the resolution of conflicts between the center and the colony, would have to come under the "informal" category. By definition, an internal colony is part of the "mother country," subject to the same laws, etc. But we have seen how the state and federal governments tend to ignore the wishes of the UP and how the State has joined with the mining and lumber industries to all but eliminate the possibility of raising necessary tax revenue through the property tax structure.

Gonzales-Casanova's last point is that the economic, political, and cultural inequalities between the two areas increase over time. In the economic sphere, the continued decline of the mining industry has spelled worsening economic woes for the UP unemployment levels hover around twelve to fifteen percent even in the best of times. As for increasing political inequalities, the best indicator is the UP's continual loss of population in the face of growing population in lower Michigan. As we have seen, from 1930 to 1970, the rest of Michigan saw a growth of 89% in its population while the UP's population declined by 4.5% (Rodefeld, 1976). This population loss represents the ebbing away of the UP's already minuscule political clout in the State Capitol. The third aspect of the sixth point is that of "increasing cultural inequality."

Gonzales-Casanova places a large measure of importance on racial, ethnic, or cultural distinctiveness between the two areas. A thorough examination of the two areas (the UP and the lower lake states) with an eye to discerning cultural differences presents problems of definition. The author admits that he is unable to identify what might be a "cultural inequality" let alone being able to discern an increase in such a commodity as satisfaction for the final aspect of Gonzales-Casanova's sixth point. (Although "true" cultural differences are not found, "surface" manifestations of culture that ordinarily and naturally accrue to industrially developed centers — such as Pittsburgh, Cleveland, Boston, and Chicago — are, with minor exceptions, absent in the Upper Peninsula. These "cultural" events include theater, dance, opera, symphony orchestras, etc.).

The UP's economy has been shown to have always been complementary to the demands for resources at the center. The irregular birth, growth, and decline of cities have been directly tied to natural resource exploitation. The UP's lack of economic integration is obvious from the "export-import" data presented on pages 25 and 26 of this thesis. Intra-peninsular transportation provides an additional case-in-point. There exist no major highways traversing the peninsula; the only existing section of interstate highway is fifty miles long and links lower Michigan with the Canadian market (from the Mackinac Bridge at St. Ignace to The International Bridge at Sault Ste. Marie). To fly from the eastern UP to the central or western UP (and vice versa), one must fly to Traverse City, Michigan or Milwaukee, Wisconsin, first.

The railroads were built almost exclusively for resource extraction. (The only clear exception was the rail from Minneapolis to Sault Ste. Marie, which will be discussed later in this study.)

We have seen that the UP's "development" was tied to resource extraction in four areas: fur, copper, lumber, and iron ore. The capital to exploit these resources came from Boston, Pittsburgh, Cleveland, and Chicago.

We explored the UP's standard of living and found that it is most likely worse than that of Appalachia. We have seen the UP's scant economic and political viability being further eroded by its declining population. We have presented and discussed Gonzales-Casanova's six points and found the UP to fit a pattern of colonial domination. We are now in a position to move to the second phase of this study: a presentation of Sault Ste. Marie's history, to see whether an individual piece of the internal colony puzzle will exhibit the same adherence to the colonial paradigm.

THE SAULT STE. MARIE EXPERIENCE

1600 to 1800: Early Colonial Outpost

For more than 300 years, Sault Ste. Marie has stood at the foot of Lake Superior and watched the wealth of an area now composed of Michigan's Upper Peninsula, northern Wisconsin and Minnesota, and northern Ontario float down the St. Marys River to points south and east.

When Etienne Brule, the first white person to see the area now called Sault Ste. Marie, came up the St. Mary's river in the 1620s, he found thousands of native people camped and fishing along what came to be called the St. Mary's rapids. Sau(l)t de Sainte Marie is French for "rapids of the St. Mary's".) These people are now called the Chippewa and the Sault was the summer meeting place of the Chippewa Nation. The rapids, formed as Lake Superior's waters fell eighteen feet to the level of Lake Huron, composed one of North America's foremost fishing grounds.

Despite this tremendous resource, most Chippewa chose to come to the rapids only for the fishing season, and perhaps as few as two hundred lived on the river year round. (It would be unfair to refer to the Chippewa's use of the area's resources as colonial exploitation since their way of life held no notion of "colony." The French, however, had a different view of the plentiful natural resources of the area.

In 1671 Sieur de Saint Lussen, on an order of King Louis XIV of France, came to Sault Ste. Marie (because of its central location amidst these holdings) to claim formal possession of the vast French holdings in North America. In a pompous ceremony in the Sault on June 4, 1671, Saint Lussen claimed "all of the vast region 'as well discovered as to be discovered' bounded on one side by the 'northern and western seas' and on the other side the Sea of the South, or the Pacific" (Bayliss and Bayliss, 1955, p. 19).

Thus began Sault Ste. Marie's role as official colonial outpost, subservient to Montreal and ultimately to the King of France. Its role as the center of French colonial activity for most of North America lasted until the end of the seventeenth century when British harassment from the north forced the French to retreat to Mackinac Island. The continuing deterioration of their influence caused the French, at the pleading of the Mackinac commandant, Antoine Cadillac, to establish a new outpost and fort at Detroit. In 1706 the French missionaries burned the mission in St. Ignace at the Straits of Mackinac, and abandoned Mackinac Island. The mission at Sault Ste. Marie had been abandoned some years before, and, as a French colonial outpost, forgotten.

With the decline of French domination of this area in the 1760s the British began exploiting the north with the same fervor shown by the French. For a while, the Sault witnessed a flurry of activities surrounding British exploitation of the fur wealth of the upper Great Lakes. But it was no longer the center of that activity; the colonial center was again at Mackinac Island. Yet Sault Ste. Marie was maintained as a trading center and held the distinction of being an important colonial outpost for British activities. After the Jay Treaty of 1794, which resolved the question of control over the North Country, the British moved their activities to the Canadian side of the St. Marys River, causing another decline in the fortune of Sault Ste. Marie.

1800 to 1880

In a short time, Sault Ste. Marie found itself embroiled in the War of 1812. John Johnston, the Sault's leading citizen and fur-trader, along with other Sault men, both Indian and white, fought on the side of the British. The British, of course, lost and the Americans burned John Johnston's house in Sault Ste. Marie, and the American Fur Company's outpost on the Canadian (British) side of the river in retaliation. Subsequently, the Americans built a fort at Sault Ste. Marie in 1822 to keep the border free of British incursion, perhaps with an eye toward keeping the errant John Johnston, an Irishman by birth, and others, in the patriotic fold.

With the Great Lakes territory firmly in American control for the first time, residents in the area began agitating for statehood. After the brief and comic Toledo War, Michigan accepted the Upper Peninsula as a concession for losing Toledo, and both peninsulas were admitted to the Union as the State of Michigan in 1837. This unnatural union brought protest from the start, and as early as 1851, the people of the UP agitated for separate statehood (Hertzel, 1976), an agitation which proceeds unabated to this day.

With statehood came exploitation and the Americans rediscovered the UP's vast copper wealth. The copper rush to the UP rivaled the gold rush to California of a few years hence. The copper activity brought expansion and prosperity to the Sault because of its location at the foot of Lake Superior.

Everything in this part of the country moved by water, and to get to and from the copper country, the rapids at the Sault had to be overcome. For many years, a lively trade was made by portaging cargo from ships in Lake Superior to ships below the rapids and vice-versa. A refinement on this theme saw whole ships being dragged on rails from one level to another. After a few false starts and much agitation in the United States Congress and the Michigan Legislature, the State of Michigan opened a lock at Sault Ste. Marie in 1855, immediately rendering obsolete the jobs of the portage laborers in the Sault. A few years later, in 1857, when an accident ruptured the lock, a call went out to the portage men of the Sault for help. They refused, striking perhaps one of the first blows in the war of the workingman against automation (Newton, 1923).

In the words of Chase Osborn, owner of the local newspaper and a future governor of Michigan, the Sault "lost much of its commercial prestige and these years (1855 to 1870) witnessed a decadence instead of an advance" (Osborn, 1887, 13).

In 1870 the federal government opened its first lock in the Sault. Because its use was toll-free and the state charged a per-ton levy for its lock, the state lock was abandoned by shippers and the state was forced to turn its lock over to the federal government. The abandonment of the state lock in deference to the federal lock is significant. Low shipping costs meant that raw materials need not be utilized in manufacture at the point of extraction. The basic raw materials of steel — iron ore, limestone, coal, and coke — comprise over 75% of all upper lakes shipping and yet the United States has no steel mills in the upper Great Lakes region (U.S. Army Corps. 1976).

1880 to 1890: The Boom Decade

The Boom of 1887 must have been one of the most colorful and exciting eras of the Sault's history. The city was incorporated in 1887 and a number of developments brought in a coven of fourteen boomers: land speculators dressed in "mink-skin coats and plug hats" (Newton, 1923). Lots offered for $25 before the boom fetched a price of $6.000. The development which brought in the boomers were: the completion of the international railroad bridge between the two Saults; four rail line companies laying track for the Sault; the Sainte Mary's Falls Water Power Company's investment of $500,000 in real estate and rights of way; the first electric street railway; city-supplied water beginning in 1886 and the running of sewer lines; the laying of gas lines; and the introduction of electricity to Sault homes.

City records show that in 1886 the value of new buildings was $43,000. In 1887, the value was $1,208,000. Population growth showed the same meteoric rise: in 1880 the Sault's population was 1,947; by 1890 it had risen to 5,760 (13th Census of the U.S., 1913). These developments prompted Chase Osborn to make the following statement and prediction: "At present (1887), the old city is enjoying a legitimate revival... (and enterprises) will make it a most important manufacturing and commercial center of large proportions" (Osborn, 1887, p. 14).

Chase Osborn offers unrelenting praise for Sault Ste. Marie, the "Mecca of the manufacturer, the capitalist...." It is both enjoyable and instructive to quote extensively from his pamphlet entitled: "The 'Soo', The New Metropolis, The Coming City of the Great Lakes, The Gem of The New North"

> Thousands of eyes have been attracted by the prominent and important location of Sault Ste. Marie, Mich., the hub of the central North, the city with a great future, surrounded, as it is, by many of the greatest advantages ever bestowed upon an earthly region... The 'Soo' with its key-like location, its grandest water-power in the world, its great locks, the bracing, cooling, exhilarating, healing atmosphere, the solidity that characterizes its present rapid growth, the coming of transcontinental railways, the hundreds of large vessels that pass its great canals daily, the vast local and governmental improvements projected and underway, its unsurpassed agricultural

resources, great forest resources, extensive mineral deposits close at hand, splendid school system and local government, elegant churches of many denominations, and many other things that constitute the foundation of a great metro-polis, will be a city of 25,000 inhabitants within three years, and its great growth will not cease or diminish. (Osborn, 1887, p. 1)

As mentioned, railroads were coming to the Sault. The first of these was the Soo Line, built by Minneapolis flour-milling capita-lists. These capitalists saw the route through the Sault and Canada as a competitive force against the rail interests in Chicago. It is indeed shorter, through the Sault, to the east from Minneapolis, and these capitalists felt the pressure of an alternate route would force lower prices upon the more southern rail lines (Soo Line Rail Road Co., 1976).

Although the railroad could be looked upon to bring a measure of prosperity to Sault Ste. Marie, it was not built with that intent. Rather it was built to serve the interests of Minneapolis capitalists. The water power syndicate is another example of outside interests coming to the Sault to exploit the natural resources. Hoping to harness the power of the rapids and bring the Sault into the industrial age, the syndicate composed of capitalists from Chicago, Wisconsin, Iowa, and Minnesota began to purchase canal rights-of-way in the 1880s (Osborn, 1887).

While calling the Sault "the Mecca of the Capitalist," Chase Osborn proceeds to list those capitalists who invested in the Sault: six from Iowa, three from Chicago, fifteen from Michigan's Lower Peninsula, and three from the Upper Peninsula (Osborn, 1887). In the words of Osborn, because of the investment these men were making in the Sault, "Sault Ste. Marie will be populous and wealthy... enter[ing] upon a phenomenal growth" (Osborn, 1887, p. 40).

1890 to 1900: Beginnings of an Industrial Age

While the Sault failed to live up to Chase Osborn's dream, the late 1880s and 1890s saw the Sault grow, while not phenomenally, certainly with an enthusiasm which bordered on the incompre-hensible. In 1900 the population soared to 10,538, up from 5,760 in 1890, making Sault Ste. Marie one of the fastest growing cities in Michigan.

Its "industrial age" was inaugurated by the establishment of the Soo Woolen Mills about 1890, the only woolen mill in the UP (Sawyer, 1911). The Woolen Mills was to supply the lumbering industry with heavy woolen clothing. The location was well chosen. Not only was Sault Ste. Marie the fastest growing major city of Michigan, Chippewa County was "the heart of the finest cattle and sheep country in the United States if not in the world" (Chipley, 1925), providing an ample source of wool.

Another industrial concern begun during this period was the Union Carbide Company. In the mid-1890s experimental work was done in Sault Ste. Marie on a process of forming calcium carbide. The company, then called the Lake Superior Carbide Company, was formed by a group of Chicago businessmen to obtain acetylene to enrich gas used to light Chicago city streets. In 1898 this company joined with the Electric Gas Company to form the Union Carbide Company (about which more will be said later in this study).

1900 to 1910: Industrial Expansion

Although it was a city of substantial size and of even more substantial promise, at the turn of the century, Sault Ste. Marie was not an industrial giant. In 1900 it was the fourth biggest Michigan city north of Bay City. It was larger than Adrien, Birmingham, Ecorse, Escanaba, Grosse Pointe, Hamtramck, Highland Park, Holland, Lincoln Park, Midland, Monroe, Mount Clemens, Pontiac, River Rouge, Royal Oak, Traverse City, Wyandotte, and Ypsilanti (U.S. Census, 1942). And of its three northern rivals, Ishpeming and Menominee were already in their decline and Alpena showed only a 4.6% growth from 1890 to 1900 (13th Census of the U.S., 1913).

Despite Sault Ste. Marie's burgeoning manufacturing potential, and its importance as a commercial and trade center, one cannot lose sight of the fact that the vast copper, iron, and timber wealth of northern Michigan only indirectly benefited the people and the communities of this vast and rich region. The bulk of the wealth followed the flowing waters of the St. Marys River and the upper Great Lakes to the lower lake states and the east. Sault Ste. Marie entered the twentieth century with construction of the world's largest tannery (built by Boston capitalists in 1900) and buoyed by the hope that the power canal under construction would bring even greater prosperity to the Sault region.

Fig. 1: Soo Woolen Mill
(Chippewa County Historical Society, Carl Materna Collection)

Fig. 2: Union Carbide Company (circa 1960)
(Chippewa County Historical Society, Carl Materna Collection)

For more than half a century, men had been able to ignore the rapids impediment to shipping, first by portaging, and now through the federal locks system. All that remained was to harness the tremendous water power. With an eighteen-foot fall, and Lake Superior as a mill pond, the power potential was staggering: enough power "to light Detroit and Chicago and all the cities lying between" (Sawyer, 1911, p. 246).

In 1902, the power canal was completed and the world's longest hydro generating plant began to produce electricity. Both the tannery and the Union Carbide Company provide clear examples of colonial exploitation. The Northwestern Leather Company factory (called "The Tannery") was built in the Sault because the Sault offered "the most advantageous location" in the whole of the United States.

The shipping of hides from the Chicago slaughterhouse did not represent an economic disadvantage when compared to the tremendous natural resources of pure water from Lake Superior and vast forests of hemlock providing tanning bark, both essential materials in the hide tanning process at that time.

One source states that raw hides came from Australia and Argentina and the tanned hides were in great demand in Europe (Sawyer, 1911). The other major concern established during this period was the Union Carbide Company. Now twenty-one on the Fortune 500, a multinational corporation with nearly five hundred plants, factories, laboratories, mines, and mills around the world, Union Carbide had its humble beginnings in Sault Ste. Marie in 1898 as the Lake Superior Carbide Company. (For the details of its formation, see page 25 of this study.)

The power canal was finished in 1902, and in 1903 Union Carbide returned to the Sault from Niagara Falls to take advantage of the canal's hydro-electric power. There was no other reason to relocate in the Sault. Coke and limestone are the raw materials from which calcium carbide is made. The coke came from the Canadian Sault and from Detroit and other lower-lake ports. The limestone came from Rogers City in lower Michigan. Coal was also needed and it too came from lower-lake ports (Bayliss and Bayliss, 1955).

Phil Bellfy

Fig. 3: Northwestern Leather Company (circa 1930)
(Chippewa County Historical Society, Carl Materna Collection)

Fig. 4: Cadillac-Soo Lumber Company
(Chippewa County Historical Society, Carl Materna Collection)

For many years, Union Carbide tried to lure a customer to the Sault to utilize the calcium carbide on site. They had no success and all of its production had to be shipped out of the Sault. Equally futile were the efforts to lure other industries besides Union Carbide to the Sault to utilize the hydro-power of the Michigan Northern Power Company. The power company consequently failed and was bought by Union Carbide, called the Union Carbide Power Company. Union Carbide continued to advertise for a factory to utilize surplus power, which, in 1920, was almost one-fourth of the total power available (Chipley, 1925).

1910 to 1940: Decline and Depression

In 1887, Chase Osborn said that Sault Ste. Marie's "great growth will not cease or diminish" (Osborn, 1887, p.l). He was wrong on both counts. In the twenty years from 1880 to 1900, the Sault's population had grown over 440%, from a frontier town of 2,000 people to a thriving, growing city of over 10,000. The years from 1900 to 1910 saw a modest growth of only 20%; and from 1910 to 1920 the Sault lost 4.1% of its population. The picture, while not nearly as rosy as Chase Osborn envisioned, was not totally dismal. The major companies continued to be viable enterprises and maintained a steady growth, and some new industries were established in the Sault during this period.

Foremost among these new companies was the Cadillac-Soo Lumber Company. Capitalized to the tune of five million dollars by downstate financiers in 1923, the Cadillac-Soo Lumber Company established the largest sawmill in the Upper Peninsula in the Sault.

In summary, in the early twenties Sault Ste. Marie had twelve factories, was served by fifteen passenger steamship lines and four rail lines, and had eight miles of street railway (Chipley, 1925). But industrial growth was nearly at a standstill and population was declining: the dream was over. In the words of a pamphlet published in 1928:

> "We (the Sault) are not trying to grow, we are trying to improve." And perhaps more poignant is this statement from the same pamphlet: "The... people who live in Sault Ste. Marie have long forgotten the time when they dreamed of a metropolis of the north, when, in their fancies, they saw skyscrapers, double boulevards, and a smoke-filled sky (Sault

News Printing Co., 1928).

Shortly after this pamphlet was written, the United States plunged into the Great Depression. And nowhere was that plunge more precipitous than in Michigan's Upper Peninsula. Three out of four people were on relief in the copper-mining county of Keweenaw; Upper Peninsula counties as a whole averaged a relief load of 33% of all families (Haber, 1935). Yet the Sault's industrial advantage over the rest of the UP permitted it to weather out the Depression in relative prosperity. Times were hard in the Sault, but no harder than in the Lower Peninsula.

1940 to 1950: The Prosperity of the War Years

At the outbreak of World War II, Sault Ste. Marie found itself in fairly good straits. The small population decline in the decade from 1910 to 1920 was reversed and in 1940, the Sault was still a fairly large and prosperous city. It was larger than Adrian, Birmingham, Ecorse, Escanaba, Grosse Pointe, Holland, Lincoln Park, Midland, Mount Clemens, Traverse City, and Ypsilanti.

And as for its northern rivals of 1900, its population outstripped the cities of Ishpeming, Menominee, and Alpena. World War II meant government contracts for both the Soo Woolen Mills and Northwestern Leather Company. Union Carbide continued its steady production of calcium carbide. The prosperity of the war years can be attested to by the employment figures for the leading Sault industries.

Northwestern Leather	850	Soo Woolen Mills	65
Union Carbide	600	Lock City Marine & Machine	200
Cadillac Soo Lumber	154	Our Own Bakery	75

Table 1: Early 1950s Employment Figures for
Sault Ste. Marie's Major Employers (various sources).

1950 to 1960: Industrial Decline

Shortly after the Korean War, the entire Michigan (and U.S.) economy began to suffer irreversible changes, changes that saw production shift from durable to non-durable goods. The first sign of this shift in the Sault community was the announcement in November of 1953 that the Soo Woolen Mills was closing because of a lack of orders. It managed to reopen but closed again in January of 1955, never again to resume production. Late in January, 1955, a group of Sault businessmen who were considering buying the mill abandoned their plans. A study conducted under their direction showed there no longer existed a market for heavy woolen goods. And woolen mills were for sale "all over the country" (*Evening News*, 1-22-55). The Soo Woolen Mill equipment was sold and the plant was razed. Sixty-five workers lost their jobs.

In another development, Northwestern Leather, the Sault's largest employer, laid off one hundred employees early in 1955 and eight more in August (*Evening News*, 3-31-55; 9-15-55).

In 1956, the Cadillac-Soo Lumber Company board met in Grand Rapids, and on March 1st they announced the Cadillac-Soo mill in the Sault would close as soon as the logs remaining in the yard were cut. They cited distance from markets and a declining wood source as reasons for the closure. The company still owned 48,000 acres in the UP; 6,000 of these acres were of virgin timber. In June of 1956 the mill closed, the equipment was sold, and the buildings were razed. Another 154 workers were unemployed. Simultaneously, on June 8, 1956, Union Carbide announced a permanent reduction of one hundred employees, offering the following explanation: "fundamental changes in the method of operation... necessarily brings about a substantial reduction in the work force" (*Evening News*, 6-8-56).

Also in 1956 (December), a joint bakery operation serving the UP and baking in Marquette, and in the Sault, ceased operating in Sault Ste. Marie and moved that portion of its production to Marquette. The company, called Our Own Bakeries, laid off most of its seventy-five Sault employees.

Lock City Marine and Machine, which repaired boat engines, and built boats and landing craft for the Army and Navy, also closed in 1956. The bakery and the Lock City Marine closures brought another 250 people into the ranks of the unemployed.

In January, 1957, the 300 to 400 workers left at Northwestern Leather ratified a new three-year contract. Faced with the staggering economic blows of 1956, the union agreed to a contract which called for "a re-evaluation of wage rates and production standards" (*Evening News*, 1-26-57). In addition to these union concessions, the city had given the tannery help in its taxes and in its power and water rates (*Evening News*, 3-25-58). During these negotiations, Northwestern Leather was sounding the same marketing alarms sounded by

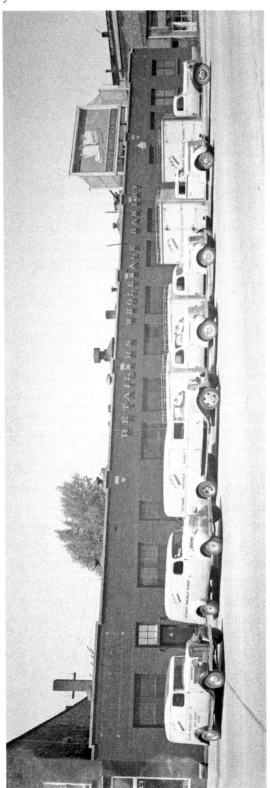

Fig. 5: Our Own Bakery
(Chippewa County Historical Society, Carl Materna Collection)

the Woolen Mills, Cadillac-Soo, and others. The timbre of these alarms was this: Sault Ste. Marie is fast losing its viability as a manufacturing center.

The January, 1957, contract allowed for either the company or the union to instigate new negotiations twelve months hence, if warranted by economic conditions. In January, 1958, the company did feel further negotiations were warranted and again called upon the union to reevaluate the wage structure and productivity standards.

Only this time, the outcome was different: the union overwhelmingly rejected the company's attempt to further erode their living standard (Evening News, 2-3-58). The company board members returned to Boston, called together the stockholders, and advised to liquidate the company. They voted to do so on February 18; the company ceased operations in mid-April and on May 7, 1958, the property and machinery were auctioned.

A Sault businessman, acting on behalf of the Sault community, and hoping to keep the tannery in operation, submitted what he felt was the highest bid for both the land and the machinery. But because of the company's interpretation of his bid and the "rules" of the auction, his bid was determined to be $5,000 short of the high bid. The company refused to reconsider his bid and the tannery was sold in pieces. The sold equipment was removed and the buildings were razed. The tannery action outraged the community and left another three hundred workers jobless (*Evening News*, 5-8-58).

Exacerbating this calamitous situation, Union Carbide, in 1958, cited high taxes, high freight rates, and increased power costs as elements creating the possibility of its closing the "Soo Works." This prompted the company to petition the city for tax relief, citing the lower taxes paid at its other calcium carbide production sites.

The Sault community viewed these Union Carbide disclosures with understandable alarm. The 1950s saw Michigan's manufacturing grow six percent while the Sault's declined sixty-three percent. The Sault's remaining production workers in late 1958 represented only 22% of its 1947 level and Union Carbide employed nearly all of those 370 production workers. The "great growth that would not cease or diminish" touted by Osborn, had ceased years ago, and the Sault's industrial strength was diminishing in earnest. The 1960 census brought the decline official status. The Sault's population in 1960 stood at 18,722, 800 more than the 1950 census, but down steeply from an estimate of 19,680 in 1957 (Thaden and Moots, 1960).

Fig. 6: Lock City Marine & Machine (Hickler Machine)
(Chippewa County Historical Society, Carl Materna Collection)

The out-migration included many people of laboring age: Sault Ste. Marie lost 14% of its labor force in the 1950s. Its 5,232 laboring age people of 1960 was actually below its 1940 figure. The manufacturing labor force in 1960 stood at 566, down from 1,545 in 1950 (Villian-Leman, 1963). In 1960, its dependency ratio revealed that for every 100 people between ages 20 and 64, there were 116 other people, compared to a 100:74 ratio for urban Michigan (Thaden and Hoots, 1960). In 1960, Michigan's unemployment rate stood at 6.9%, Sault Ste. Marie's at 12.8%.

The new decade found the once-proclaimed "gem of the new north" in seriously hard times. The nearly 150-year association with the federal military also showed signs of decline: Fort Brady closed in late 1945, the Navy hydrological station closed in 1954, and on March 29, 1960, the Army's Camp Lucas closed, transferring 610 military personnel out of the Sault and adding another one hundred civilian employees to the Sault's swelling ranks of unemployed (KISS, 1976).

1960 to 1970: The End of the Industrial Age

Union Carbide produced (among many other products) calcium carbide, which, when mixed with water, released acetylene gas. Acetylene was the chemical source of the early plastics industry. Bayliss and Bayliss, in their book, *River of Destiny* (1955), sing the praises of acetylene: synthetic organic chemicals produced from acetylene figure in the manufacture of sulfa drugs and other pharmaceuticals, lacquers for coating automobiles, photographic supplies, dyes, and dry-cleaning fluids... synthetic rubber and aspirin." (Bayliss and Bayliss, p. 148). They state that the uses of acetylene are "almost unlimited."

In 1955, the future of acetylene looked bright indeed, but by the late 1950s, chemists were discovering that natural gas could be substituted for acetylene in the plastics and related industries. It was during this period that Union Carbide began to complain that the substitution of natural gas for acetylene was affecting the marketability of calcium carbide, the Soo Works Works' only product.

On February 22, 1961, the Union Carbide Company issued a statement which said, in part, "Tax relief... is absolutely essential to have a chance of becoming competitive and obtaining and holding new markets." That plea fell on the deaf ears of the city fathers, and on August 1, 1962, Union Carbide announced the closure of the Sault plant. Most of the reasons listed were well known to Sault residents: distance from markets, high taxes, high freight rates, and the reduction of power output due to lower water levels in Lake Superior. Union Carbide's closure dealt the death-blow to the Sault's Industrial Age. The company that dominated the Sault's industrial scene for sixty years was leaving, taking with it a tax base that paid nearly 30% of all the taxes levied by Chippewa County and the City of Sault Ste. Marie. (Sault Ste. Marie is the county seat of Chippewa County.) They laid off 270 workers whose average service to the company was about twenty-five years (*Evening News*, 8-1-62).

Union Carbide officially ceased its operations in the Sault on November 30, 1963. They sold the canal and power generating plant to Edison-Soo Electric Company, the local electric utility, which was owned by investors in St. Louis. The carbide plant equipment was either moved to other Union Carbide operations or sold, and the buildings were razed to reduce Union Carbide's property tax levies.

The 1970 census data records the serious toll the industrial decline had taken on the Sault area in the previous decade. The steady population loss of the late 1950s was accelerated. The Sault's population fell to 15,136, a level previously attained sometime in the late 1930s. Its non-worker ratio soared to 1.70. At the same time, surrounding Chippewa County suffered a net loss of 19.7% through migration as more working-age people moved out of the county.

During the 1960s, employment in the United States grew 23.4%, while total employment in Chippewa County actually declined slightly. The big employment losers were agriculture, forestry and fisheries, down 73%, and manufacturing, down 49%. The loss in the manufacturing sector occurred at the same time the U.S. manufacturing sector grew 13.6%. The only area that showed any substantial growth was the public administration area, up 21% from 1960. And yet, even this growth was 10% behind the public administration growth rate for the United States as a whole (KISS, 1976).

Synthesis

Many would believe that the preceding data forces a locational explanation upon the problems of Sault Ste. Marie. There is no lack of official company statements to that effect: Cadillac-Soo Lumber, Northwestern Leather, Union Carbide, and Our Own Bakeries all complained of marketing and transportation problems.

Yet upon closer examination, it seems that location factors fail to explain the entire relationship between the eastern Upper Peninsula and the industrial demands of the United States. We must attempt to discern the underlying pattern of underdevelopment that created the boom and bust of the Sault area; in this way the Gonzales-Casanova pattern of exploitation becomes evident.

The lock system was in no way intended to serve the interests of the Sault; indeed, it had the opposite effect: from its inception it was intended to move goods through the Sault faster and cheaper. The first railroad to the Sault was not intended to serve the Sault, but was built as a route *through* the city, again intending to serve outside interests. The lumbering era of Chippewa County and of the entire UP did not serve the people of the area: the intention was to exploit the area's timber resources.

The Sault's industrial era mirrors this exploitative pattern. Northwestern Leather was here to exploit the pure water and forest resources; Union Carbide to exploit the cheap hydro-electric power;

Cadillac-Soo, the lumber resources. All the industrial concerns that abandoned the area sold their equipment to outside interests and razed their factory buildings, insuring that local control and/or operations would be completely impossible. Northwestern Leather and Union Carbide did leave something behind: a legacy of toxic wastes.

The tannery site, completely devoid of buildings, is nonetheless laced with toxins, including arsenic, cyanide, mercury, lead, and chromium. The chromium and cyanide are both found in concentrations in excess of Environmental Protection Agency standards (*Evening News*, 10-24-80). In a testament to understatement, the *Evening News* states: "It [the original tannery owners]... have left the Sault and chances of their being forced to come back and clean up the site may be very slim" (*Evening News*, 10-24-80, p. 1).

Acetylene gas is produced by mixing calcium carbide and water — the by-product of this chemical process is calcium hydroxide, or lime. Union Carbide disposed of this by-product by merely piling it near their plant. This 375,000 cubic yard mountain, "given" to the city when Union Carbide left the Sault, is in many places chemically active just below the surface and poses a serious threat to the children who play on and around the pile.

Following an article in the Sault Evenings News on October 20, 1980, public concern became acute. The newspaper reported the findings of a Michigan Department of Natural Resources (MDNR) investigation which found unusually high concentrations of cyanide in the pile which may pose threat to ground water supplies. The Union Carbide ad slogan of a few years back — "Today, something we do will touch your life" — has taken on a new meaning for Sault residents in light of the MDNR findings.

The full potential of the health threat posed by both the tannery and the Union Carbide wastes is yet to be realized. Yet it seems clear that these and the other companies, who moved from Sault Ste. Marie, did so with very little regard for the local economy and with even less regard for the area's people.

To place the colonial designation and the concomitant economic factors in clearer perspective, one need only look across the St. Marys River from Sault Ste. Marie, Michigan, to Sault Ste. Marie, Ontario. The UP's colonial status has resulted in a radically different form of development for the American Sault when compared to the Canadian Sault.

The Sault Ste. Marie, Ontario, Experience

In 1901, when the Sault was a thriving city of over 10,000 people, Sault Ste. Marie, Ontario, was a city of 7,169, and this difference was maintained until the early teens of the century. However, in the decade from 1910 to 1920, the Michigan Sault lost 4.1% of its population, while Sault, Ontario, nearly doubled its population, growing from 10,984 in 1911 to 21,092 in 1921.

More recent comparison of the two Saults continues this startling contrast. In the early 1950s, Sault, Ontario's Algoma Steel Corporation employed about 7,000 people. At the time, its steel mill was the largest in all of Canada (Bayliss and Bayliss, 1955). The Abitibi Power and Paper Company, utilizing Lake Superior water power and northern Ontario timber to produce newsprint, employed over 600 people. At this time (1951), the Canadian Sault supported a population of 32,452 (Sault, Michigan: 17,912). In the fifties — the decade of Sault, Michigan's precipitous industrial decline — the Algoma District (Sault, Ontario its major city) showed a manufacturing growth rate of between ten and twenty percent, and a population gain of over 25% (Dean, 1969).

Sault Michigan's decline is nearly as powerful as the growth of Sault, Ontario. Sault, Michigan's population fell 19% in the 1960s; Sault, Ontario's grew 44% in this same period, to 76,000, in 1969. The seventies saw Sault, Michigan's population decline to 14,039 (1980 census figures), while Sault, Ontario's grew to an estimated 81,000 in 1978 (Squiqna, 1978). The industrial strength of Sault, Ontario, can be seen by the fact that, with Sarnia, Ontario, Canadian Sault industrial workers earned 50% to 75% more than the average Ontario wage earner (Dean, 1969).

The essential difference in the history of the Saults is that while the Upper Peninsula's resources were being exploited, northern Ontario's resources were being utilized at the point of extraction. The resources are the same on either shore of Lake Superior: iron ore, timber, and water power. But while these resources brought people and prosperity to Sault, Ontario, they brought neither to Sault, Michigan.

Fig. 7: Algoma Steel Mill, 1954
(http://www.cityssm.on.ca/library/Clergue/

It should be apparent that the standard capitalist geographic argument used to explain the economics of the eastern Upper Peninsula falls flat when voiced with a knowledge of Sault, Ontario's history. Distance from markets and transportation problems cease to be problems when considering Sault Ontario's place within the Canadian economy. Sault, Ontario, is as far from its major market areas — Toronto and Montreal — as Sault Michigan is from its major markets.

The fact that Sault, Ontario, is at the U.S. border and situated in the middle of Canada's only east-west transportation route insures that, despite its distance from markets, it will remain within Canada's industrial core, albeit on the periphery. It would be impossible to explain how two cities, a river-width apart, both equidistant from their supposed markets, and with identical "transportation problems" and with identical resources could result in two radically different economies unless there exists underlying structural components, which forced the cities to take different paths to "development."

Sault, Ontario, emerges as a partner to Canadian industry, sharing in the benefits accruing to industrialization, while the American Sault's picture traces a path in history from a colonial trade center, through a neo-colonial industrial age, and into the decline and decay in which it finds itself today.

The 1970s: The Decline Continues

What has been related thus far has been in terms of history, but if the colonial appellation is valid, present conditions must continue to reflect this relationship. Official unemployment figures for Chippewa County since the closing of Union Carbide's Soo Works run the range of 11.2% in the "good" year of 1966 to an average of 21.8% for the first six months of 1979. The 1979 figures also show a loss of about 7.5% of the area's civilian labor force since January. Unofficial estimates of the unemployment rate during the recession year of 1975 were placed at nearly 30% (KISS, 1976). Using the latest figures available, the unemployment rate for December, 1980, in Chippewa County was 22.6%. 1980 Census figures complete the dismal picture. Chippewa County lost 13.1% of its 1970 population, which stands at 28,158. Sault Ste. Marie was down 7% to 14,039, equal to its population during the early 1930s (Evening News, 7-22-80).

Fig. 8: **Abitibi Power & Paper; Sault, Ontario** (circa 2012)
((https://www.flickr.com/photos/68678468@N06/7940288708/)

Closures and loss of jobs still dominate the employment picture of the Sault and the surrounding area. In the closing months of 1977, the U.S. Air Force phased out its operation at Kincheloe Air Force Base (KAFB), 18 miles south of the Sault. One source prior to the closing estimated the employment loss for Chippewa County could be as high as 2,700 jobs. This would have meant that more than one out of every four workers would lose his or her job.

The closure of KAFB did not result in the severe economic problem that was anticipated, because of a blitzkrieg move by the State of Michigan, which converted barracks housing on the base into a medium security prison that became operational on February 1, 1978, employing approximately 250 area people. Thus the 1978 unemployment figures show a rise of only about 2% for 1977 to 18.0% for 1978.

Coming close on the heels of the Kincheloe closing was an announcement by Essex Wire that it was closing its wiring harness assembly plant in Sault Ste. Marie. The Essex experience is highly reminiscent of a third world country's experience with an industrial multinational. The city lured Essex Wire to Sault Ste. Marie by granting them a five-year tax break at a site in the Municipal Industrial Park. A slowdown in the auto industry delayed the opening of the plant for almost two years, eating up two years of their five-year tax break period. The city refused to extend this tax break period.

About three years after beginning production and near the end of their tax break period, Essex Wire issued a statement citing shipping costs, foreign competition, and high turnover at the Sault plant as problems confronting its operation (Evening News, 9-7-78). Union negotiations were then underway for a new three-year contract, replacing one that was to expire on September 27, 1978. The workers, receiving ten cents per hour more than minimum wage, were demanding a substantial wage increase. (The company's statement was in response to this contract demand.)

On September 14, 1978 (*Evening News*), Essex, the city's largest private employer, announced that it was closing, and on September 22, 1978, it discontinued operations, throwing 250 more workers into the ranks of the unemployed. Community sentiment expressed the belief that without the tax break and its near minimum-wage pay rate, Essex didn't care to remain in the Sault and intended to find another city with high unemployment and an advantageous tax rate to exploit.

The Essex Wire experience, while tragic, is in imitation of the area's pattern of exploitation. In this case, the resources to be exploited are not the natural resources of timber, iron ore, or copper, but those of low tax rates and an impoverished work force willing to accept a job-rate at half of what the same job would demand in the "mother country," near Detroit. Samir Amin places such experiences firmly within the colonial context. He points out that if "a resource (in this case, impoverished workers)... is suddenly opened up... (attracting) a large influx of foreign capital, and... the tax burden... can be increasingly lightened... miracle growth" may visit an area (Amin, 1976, p. 291).

But, again, Amin points out that this growth is not development, but rather the development of underdevelopment. The Essex closing is a final testament to this colonial exploitation. The Essex pattern will be repeating itself, as company after company explores the possibility of locating in the Sault area, enticed by various government-funded "development corporations" with the lure of low interest loans, low rents, tax breaks, and destitute, but eager workers.

INTERNAL COLONY

We have seen the upper Great Lakes region's fur-bearing animals harvested to scarcity; copper mined so fiercely that within one hundred years, 9.6 billion pounds were shipped out of the UP (now only one mine continues to produce); feverish iron mining that saw 1.2 trillion pounds of ore shipped from 1900 to 1951 (today only four mines still produce); extensive lumbering, with over one billion board feet shipped by 1926, leaving ten million acres devastated.

In the copper industry, we saw that the Calumet and Hecla Mining Company of Boston shipped 48% of all copper shipped out of the UP from 1846 to 1946; in the iron ore industry, 1 in 1950, 67% of all mines were controlled by companies headquartered in Cleveland; in 1910, 47% of the total UP land area was owned by thirty-two holders; and at the end of the fur era, all trading throughout the entire region was controlled by one man.

The wealth shipped out of the Upper Peninsula was enormous; the estimated value of lumber shipped or wasted: $1 billion; the value of copper shipped by 1950: $1.5 billion; the value of the iron ore shipped between 1900 and 1951: $3.8 billion; and the value of the UP's decimated fur resource: inestimable.

And what has this vast wealth accomplished for the people of the Upper Peninsula? Sometime during the 1920s, the UP population began to decline, and it has been declining ever since. The period from 1930 to 1970 saw the UP lose 4.5% of its population. And in the wake of this declining population, is a picture of poverty that rivals the dismal vistas of Appalachia.

How does the Sault Ste. Marie experience compare with that for the Upper Peninsula as a whole? Northwestern Leather, a Boston company, located in the Sault in order to utilize the resources of tanning bark and pure water, and left a legacy of heavy metal waste; Union Carbide, a powerful multinational, came to the Sault to utilize its cheap hydro-power , and left behind a 375,000 cubic yard lime pile laced with deadly cyanide; the Cadillac-Soo Lumber Company established the UP's largest sawmill in the Sault to utilize the last of the area's timber resources; Essex Wire was in the Sault only long enough to take advantage of municipal tax breaks and cheap labor: when these two resources ran out, so did Essex.

So what happened to the UP and Sault Ste. Marie when the resources dwindled? The companies left, taking their fortunes and the livelihood of thousands of families with them. They left in their wake dislocation, massive unemployment, a raped environment, persistent poverty, and social costs too great to imagine.

Clearly the UP/Sault experience mirrors that of a colony in the classic sense. Indeed, the data presented certainly support Al Gedicks when he writes of the upper Great Lakes region as a resource colony and leads one to an acceptance of Gonzales-Casanova's internal colony designation as well, even though Gonzales-Casanova is concerned that the term may be used "in a vague, emotional, irrational, or aggressive way" (Gonzales-Casanova, 1965, p. 121). Yet it may be some of those very qualities which impart to the internal colony notion a large measure of utility.

As D. L. Johnson explains, there exists within the notion of internal colony a quality that contains "a sense of magnitude and urgency (and having) the potential to awaken whatever humanity remains in man, of broadening consciousness, of stimulating action for developmental change" (Johnson, 1972, p.30l).

It is precisely this national liberation implication that leads this author to the "internal colony" appellation when speaking about the Upper Peninsula. It is with Johnson's "sense of urgency" that the UP has been studied within the colonial context, and the "potential for broadening consciousness" has forced a careful scrutiny of the Sault's experience. It is hoped that the resultant study will encourage people to look upon the Upper Peninsula as less of a State Park and Resource Center and more as an "emerging nation" with goals and aspirations yet to be realized.

NEW CONCLUSION

If I were to title this chapter following the format of my Thesis, I would have to title it: "1980 to 2018: The Decline Continues."

Iron Mining

There is only one iron-ore mine still in operation in the UP — the Tilden Mine — near Ishpeming. Its "sister mine," the Empire, ceased operation in 2016. The Tilden Mine employs about 770 workers.

Nickel and Copper Mining

There is one "copper" mine operating in the UP — the controversial "Eagle Project," located in the "Yellow Dog Plains," north of Marquette. It really should be called a "nickel-copper mine," as it is projected to produce more nickel concentrates than copper per year (17k tons, versus 13k tons). The Project was controversial from the start due to serious environmental concerns, and even more serious concerns by American Indians, who view "Eagle Rock" as sacred. The mining shaft is located in an area that will all but ensure the desecration of this Sacred Site.

There are several other mines being proposed for the UP, all of them are being opposed by environmentalists. The opposing sentiment is typified by a "Quit Whining and Start Mining" bumper-sticker mentality.

Regardless of your view of "hard-rock" mining in the UP, none of the mines currently operating employ significant numbers of workers. The Tilden Mine employs about 770 people. The owners of the Eagle mine claim that it employs about 200 people, although the environmental group "Save the Wild UP" claims the number is closer to 80. For comparison, in its heyday (1917), UP copper and iron ore mines employed more than 20,000 people; today, being generous, the number is about 900.

Timber Resource Utilization

There is nothing operating on the scale of the Cadillac-Soo Lumber Company anywhere in the UP today. There are three UP "specialty" mills, though: Ottawa Forest Products, operating mills in Ironwood and Amassa, and Superior Sawmill, with one mill in Trenary. There are a number of small mills operating throughout the UP, utilizing local timber resources.

The "UP Paper" mill in Manistique doesn't use timber for its mill; their website says that they manufacture "100% recycled kraft paper." Today, the Dunn Paper mill in Menominee employs about 100 people. It has closed and reopened several times in its history.

Statistics from 2013 (most recent available) for forestry-related jobs in the UP show about 1300 people are employed in this industry sector.

Sault Ste. Marie, Michigan, 2018

Returning to our focus on the "Twin Saults," we see Sault Michigan's population continuing its downward trajectory. As we've seen, the Sault's population reached a peak of about 20,000 (p.41). It now stands at 13,631 (2018, US Census estimate); in 2010, the census Bureau pegged it at 14,144, a loss of 3.6%.

The Sault's population "source of income" shows that over 60% comes from Social Security, public assistance, supplemental assistance, or retirement investments. Its "long-term" unemployment rate is 9.35%, although it is currently estimated to be at 6.7% (June 2018).

Manufacturing employment stands at 6.2% (compared to a rate of 10.4% for the US). Adding all "extractive industry" employment figures, the rate rises to about 7.2%, also far below the federal "extractive industry" average of over 12%. "Health care and social assistance" accounts for 18.8%, the largest income sector in Sault Michigan's economy.

Overall, the Sault, Michigan, economic picture is still quite bleak — an older and aging population relying on "retirement income" living in a community with little opportunity, a trend that started with the end of its industrial era, starting in the late '50s, and continuing unabated since that time.

The "prison complex" that once comprised five facilities at the former Kincheloe AFB, shrunk to two, as of late 2015. Employment figures, both historic and current, could not be found, but the shuttering of prisons almost always results in a loss of jobs. Michigan has closed or merged 26 facilities since 2005. In 2006, the state had 51,454 prisoners; in 2017 that number dipped below 40,000.

Sault Ste. Marie, Ontario, 2018

For all of its touted supremacy over its "Michigan Sister City," Sault, Ontario, has also witnessed a decline in its "industrial might." This decline may work against some of the arguments I made in my Thesis (the first 52 pages of this book), but I will leave the reader to make that conclusion. My argument today is that the industrial decline of Sault, Ontario, may be a direct result of "globalization," and much less a result of any "core-periphery" tension.

While all of Sault Michigan's industry was shuttered by 1970, it took decades longer for Sault Ontario to feel the ravages of de-industrialization.

Abitibi Paper Mill

Most of the buildings comprising the Abitibi Paper Mill were demolished in late 2012. The property awaits "redevelopment" as of this writing. The mill was called St. Marys Paper at the time of its closing and demolition.

Essar Steel Algoma Mill

In this continuing "steel mill saga," on August 2, 2018, Essar Steel Algoma announced that it was selling the mill to unnamed investors, with the name returning to the simple Algoma Steel. This sale comes 30 months after Essar filed for bankruptcy protection. The mill had fallen on "hard times," indeed. Down from its peak employment of about 7000 in the 1950s, (3500 in 2008), Algoma Steel employs 2,700 people, as of this writing.

Phil Bellfy

Fig. 9: Former Kincheloe AFB, 2006
(prisons are located just right of center, on south side of the east-west road)

Fig. 10: Abitibi paper mill site after demolishment, 2012 ((International Bridge in the background).

Internal Colony Redux

Let us now return to the Gonzales-Casanova's formulation of an "Internal Colony" and see how the designation has stood up over the past 40 years. To remind the readers, this formulation has its roots in the concept that the dominant power maintains a monopoly over the client region in the areas of exploitation of natural resources, labor-force utilization, import-export trade, and the distribution of revenue from these activities. The salient features of these monopolies consist of the following:

1. The economy of the internal colony is structured to complement that of the colonial center. Specifically, the exploitation of a natural resource is a function of the demand for that resource at the center. This inevitably leads to a distorted development of colonial sectors and regions, most often reflected in the irregular birth and growth of cities. This distorted development is further reflected in the lack of economic integration in the interior of the colony, coupled with the lack of cultural integration and communication. This aspect of the "Internal Colony" formulation remains true today (2018).

2. The internal colony in question has its "development" tied to a predominant sector, i.e. mining or agriculture, and to a predominant product within that sector, for example, iron ore or cocoa. This "specialization" leads to various forms of internal colonies. These monopolies may concentrate in fiscal areas, natural exploitation, foreign trade, etc. This is true, today: the areas of mining, wood products, and paper manufacturing in the UP show "location quotients" of 17 for mining, 7 for wood products, and 6 for paper manufacturing. The "LQ" ratio compares the concentration of employment in the "colonial region" when compared to the core.

3. In order to maintain the monopoly structure, one would expect to find that the land, water, and/or mining concessions are granted only to interests within the one colonial center. Well, this aspect has taken an interesting turn; with the exception of the Tilden mine, owned by Cleveland Cliffs, all of the operating or proposed mines are owned by "foreign

investors," mostly Canadian ventures.

4. We should discover an obvious disparity in the standards of living between the colony and its center. Per-capita income (from the 2010 Census) for UP counties ranges from a high of $23,854 for Dickinson County (#21), to a low of $17,195 for Luce County, which is ranked 82 out of the 83 Michigan counties. The Michigan average is $25,135 (13 counties are above that average; all UP counties show below average per-capita income levels).

5. Resolutions of class conflicts resulting from these disparities will be regulated by a repressive conflict-resolution structure (either formal or informal). There's really no data on either side of this aspect of the "Internal Colony" formulation; that is, there doesn't seem to be any evidence of "class-conflict," perhaps because there doesn't don't seem to be wide disparities of wealth in the UP (see #4, above), although in the US as a whole, the gap between the "haves" and the "have-nots" is the highest of any industrialized nation in the world.

6. Over time, the center-internal colony system has a tendency to increase the economic, political, and cultural inequalities existing between the two areas. This seems to be true today all across the UP: unemployment rates are always above the state average. In June of 2018, the statewide average was 4.3%; for the UP, the unemployment rate stood at 5.5%. Historically, the rates have been much more divergent (and, often, much higher). And, in order to understand the employment / unemployment numbers, one must consider the make-up of the UP population.

First, consider that Michigan was the only state in the union shown to have lost population in the 2010 Census, and, since 2010, 14 of the UP's 15 counties have seen further population loss. Only Keweenaw County had a net population gain of 43 (to 2199), a 2% growth since the 2010 Census. At the other end of the spectrum, Ontonagon showed a loss of 869 people, a loss of more than one in eight.

With the exception of the three counties with state universities (Houghton, Marquette, and Chippewa), the other UP counties have median ages of about 50. For comparison, Michigan's overall median age is about 40 (which, in turn, is about two years older than the national average). And, it is important to note that Michigan as a whole has "aged" four years since 2000. This older and shrinking population is directly related to the loss of jobs and opportunity in the state, with younger people moving where the jobs are (or to where those jobs are perceived to be).

So, simply based on this admittedly 2018 cursory survey of the available statistics, and a reexamination of the Gonzales-Casanova paradigm, it appears that the UP is still the "Internal Colony" that it was in 1980. "Resource exploitation" is still the only game in town (although greatly diminished in its ferocity). And both of the "Twin Saults" are still struggling from serious and widening "core-periphery" disparities.

Concluding Remarks

As this book goes to press, the United States seems to be at the beginning stages of a trade war, which will indeed affect the "Twin Saults." Algoma Steel (its "new" 2018 post-sale name) faces an uncertain future as President Trump announced a 25% tariff on imported steel, including steel from Canada. Business leaders and politicians on both sides of the border that separates the "Twin Saults" have expressed grave concern over the imposed tariffs on steel, and many other goods, and the threat these tariffs pose to "cross-border" trade.

About the Author

Phil Bellfy, PhD, is the Editor and Publisher of the Ziibi Press, Enrolled Member of the White Earth Band of Minnesota Chippewa, Co-Director of the Center for the Study of Indigenous Border Issues (CSIBI), and Professor Emeritus of American Indian Studies, Michigan State University. He has been involved in environmental issues, at the Tribal, international, national, state, and local levels for over 45 years. He is also a Lay Advocate, qualified and admitted to practice Tribal Law in the Courts of the Sault Ste. Marie Tribe of Chippewa Indians.

About the Ziibi Press

The Ziibi Press is the publishing arm of CSIBI. "Ziibi" is the Ojibway word for "river," as in Mississippi (Ki-chi-ziibi; "a really big river"). CSIBI is focused on the political, economic, and cultural boundaries that separate Indigenous People from each other and the elements of the more dominant societies, much like a "really big river."

2018 – Sault Ste. Marie's Semiseptennial

It should be noted that the 2018 publication date of this book (and the year that much of its "new conclusion" data was collected) marks the 350th anniversary of the establishment of a Jesuit mission in the Sault, supporting its claim to be the third oldest city in the US.

Visit our website <ZiibiPress.com>
for information on our other publications.

BIBLIOGRAPHY

(Showing original Thesis sources; 2018 "New Conclusion" data taken from US or Michigan government websites or established news sources.)

Amin, S. (1976). *Unequal development.* London: Monthly Review Press. Translated by Brian Pearce. New York: Monthly Review Press.

Bayliss, J. & Bayliss, E.L. (1955). *River of destiny: The St. Mary's.* In collaboration with Milo M. Quaife. Detroit: Wayne State University Press. Author's note: This book was reprinted in 2018 by the Chippewa County Historical Society as part of the Sault's Semiseptennial "remembrance" of its founding by Jesuit missionaries.

Beeson, L & Lemmer, V.F. (1966). *The effects of the civil war on mining in Michigan.* Lansing: Michigan Civil War Centennial Observance Committee.

Catton, B. (1976). *Michigan: A bicentennial history.* New York: W. W. Norton and Co. Chipley, C. E. 1925

"Sault Ste. Marie." Pamphlet compiled by C. E. Chipley. Sault Ste. Marie: Evening News.

CALA, (1974). "Newsletter of the Community Action on Latin America." Madison, Wisc. Vol. 4, No.2.

Dean, W. G. (ed.) (1969). *Economic atlas of ontario.* Toronto: University of Toronto Press.

Dodge, R.L. (1973). *Michigan ghost towns: Upper peninsula.* Troy, Mich.: Glendon Publishing Co.

Drier, R.W., & DuTemple, O.J. (1961). *Prehistoric copper mining in the Lake Superior region: A collection of reference articles.* Calumet, Mich. Published by the authors.

Duncombe, B.F. (1962). "Upper Midwest Commodity Flows." Technical Paper No. 4. Minneapolis: Upper Midwest Research and Development Council and The University of Minnesota.

The Evening News: Sault Ste. Marie, Michigan. Cited the following dates: 1-22-55; 3-31-55; 9-15-55; 6-8-56; 1-26-57; 2-3-58; 3-25-58; 5-8-58; 8-1-62; 11-18-77; 9-7-78; 9-14-78; 7-10-80; 7-22-80; 10-20-80; 10-24-80.

Frank, A.G. (1972). "The Development of Underdevelopment." In James D. Cockcroft, Andre Gunder Frank and Dale L. Johnson, *Dependence and underdevelopment*. Garden City, N.Y.: Anchor Books.

Galtung, J. (1971). A Structural Theory of Imperialism. *Journal of Peace Research,* 8(2), 81–117.

Garrison, A. (1966). "Sault Ste. Marie; Economic Future and History." *Michigan State Economic Record* 8:1-3.

Gates, W. B. (1951). *Michigan cooper and Boston dollars, an economic history of the Michigan copper mining industry.* Cambridge: Mass., Harvard University Press.

Gedicks, A. (1973). "Guerrilla Research: Reversing the Machinery." *Journal of Applied Behavioral Science* 9: 645-663.

Gedicks, A. (1976a). "A Proposal for the Establishment of a Center for Alternative Mining Development Policy." Madison, Wisc.: Community Action on Latin America.

Gedicks, A. (1976b). "Copper Country Chippewas: A Tribe Joins the Third World." *The Nation* 227:582-584.

Gilbert, J.C. and Harris, C.K (1978). "Corporate Land Ownership and Rural Poverty: A Center-Periphery Model Applied to the Upper Peninsula of Michigan." Paper presented at the Annual Meeting of the Rural Sociological Society, San Francisco, Sept. 1-3, 1978.

Gonzales-Casanova, P. (1965). "Internal Colonialism and National Development". Studies in *Comparative International Development,* 1(4), 27-37.

Haber, W., & Stanchfield, P. L. (1935). *Unemployment and relief in Michigan.* Lansing: MI.

Hertze1, L.J. (1976). "Dreams of Statehood". *North American Review,* 261(2), 18-28.

Johnson, D.L. (1972). "Dependence and the International System." In James D. Cockcroft, Andre Gunder Frank and Dale L.

Johnson; *Dependence and underdevelopment*. Garden City, N.Y.: Anchor Books.

Johnson, D.L. (1972a). "On Oppressed Classes." In James D. Cockcroft, Andre Gunder Frank and Dale L. Johnson, Dependence and Under-development. Garden City, N.Y.: Anchor Books.

Johnson, I.A. (1919). *The michigan fur trade*. Lansing: Michigan Historical Commission.

KISS (1976). "Kincheloe Air Force Base Impact Special Study." Unpublished study conducted by Lake Superior State College, Sault Ste. Marie, Michigan.

LSIOA 1952 Lake Superior Iron Ores: Mining Directory and Statistical Record of the Lake Superior Iron Ore District of the United States and Canada. 2nd ed. Cleveland: Lake Superior Iron Ore Association.

Loomis, R. A. and M. E. Wirth 1967 "An Economic Survey of the Northern Lake States Region." U.S.D.A. Agricultural Economic Report no. 108. East Lansing: Michigan State University Agricultural Experiment Station Economic Research Service.

M.D.N.R. (1976). "Michigan Mineral Producers, 1976." Lansing: Michigan Department of Natural Resources.

Michigan's UP Poverty; Jobless Rate Matches Appalachia. (1964, March 3). *Wall Street Journal*, p. 1.

Newton, S. (1923). The Story of Sault Ste. Marie and Chippewa County. Sault Ste. Marie: Sault News Printing Co.

N.M.U. (1965). Manpower Problems and Economic Opportunities in an Adjusting Regional Economy: The Upper Peninsula of Michigan. Marquette, Mich.: Northern Michigan University.

Osborn, C.S. (ed.) (1887) *The 'soo': Scenes in and about sault ste. marie, michigan*. Milwaukee: King, Fowle and Katz.

Rodefeld, R.D. (1976). Unpublished data. Michigan State University, Dept. of Sociology.

Sault News Printing Co. (1928). "Homecoming Program and Souvenir of Sault Ste. Marie and Chippewa County." Sault

Ste. Marie, Mich.

Sawyer, A,C. (1911). A History of the Northern Peninsula of Michigan and Its People. Chicago: Lewis Publishing Co.

Smith, B.F. (1974). "Latifundia in Gitchegumee." Chapter 1 and 15 of a forthcoming book, *The prime principles*. Ada, Mich.: The Abadile Press.

Soo Line Rail Road Company. (1976). "Soo Liner". Bicentennial issue of company newsletter. Minneapolis, Minn.

Sparhawk, W.N. & Brush, W.D. (1929). "The Economic Aspects of Forest Destruction in Northern Michigan." U.S. Dept. of Agriculture Technical Bulletin no. 92, Washington, D.C.

Squiqna, V.M. (1978). "An Introduction to Sault Ste. Marie, Ontario, Canada." Sault Ste."Marie, Ontario: Dept. of Economic Development.

Strassmann, W.P. (1958). *Economic growth in northern michigan*. East Lansing: Michigan State University Institute for Community Development.

Thaden, J.F. & Moots, B. (1960). *The people of sault ste. marie, michigan*. East Lansing: Michigan State University Institute for Community Development. c. 1960.

U.S. Army Corps of Engineers. (1976). Soo Locks unpublished traffic reports. Sault Ste. Marie, Mich.

U.S. Bureau of Census. (1942). Sixteenth Census of the United States. Washington, D.C.: Dept. of Commerce.

U.S. Bureau of Census. (1913). Thirteenth Census of the United States. Washington, D.C.; Dept. of Commerce.

U.S. Department of Commerce. (1913). *The lumber industry*. Washington, D.C.

U.P. Statehood. (1975, June 9). *Washington Post*, p. 10.

Vilican-Leman and Associates, Inc. (1963) "A Master Plan Report for the City of Sault Ste. Marie, Michigan; Planning Report No.5: Economic Base Analysis." Southfield, Mich.

INDEX

Toltec, 11
toxic waste, 21, 22
unemployment, 7, 23
Union Carbide, 32, 35, 38, 39,
   44
  closure, 44
  layoff, 40
Union Carbide Power Company,

38
War of 1812, 11, 28
War of Independence, 12
wetlands, 21, 22
Wisconsin, 6, 18, 21, 27, 31
World War II, 19, 39
Yellow Dog Plains, 55

CPSIA information can be obtained
at www.ICGtesting.com
Printed in the USA
BVHW041007140921
616364BV00016B/30